poets
IN view

a visual anthology of 50 classic poems

CHRIS EMERY was born in Manchester in 1963 and studied painting and printmaking in Leeds. He is Publishing Director of Salt in Cambridge, England. His poetry has appeared in numerous journals including *The Age*, *Jacket*, *Magma*, *Poetry London*, *Poetry Review*, *Poetry Wales*, *PN Review* and *The Rialto*. A first full-length collection, *Dr. Mephisto* (Arc Publications) appeared in 2002, his latest collection is *Radio Nostalgia* (Arc Publications, 2006). He is also the author of a bestselling writer's guide, *101 Ways to Make Poems Sell* (Salt Publishing, 2006). He lives in Great Wilbraham with his wife, three children and various other animals.

Also by Chris Emery

POETRY
  Dr. Mephisto (Arc Publications, 2002)
  Radio Nostalgia (Arc Publications, 2006)

WRITER'S GUIDE
  101 Ways to Make Poems Sell (Salt Publishing, 2006)

poets IN view

a visual anthology of 50 classic poems

Edited by
CHRIS emery

SALT

CAMBRIDGE

PUBLISHED BY SALT PUBLISHING
PO Box 937, Great Wilbraham, Cambridge CB21 5JX United Kingdom

Selection and introduction © Chris Emery, 2008

The right of Chris Emery to be identified as the
editor of this work has been asserted by him in accordance
with Section 77 of the Copyright, Designs and Patents Act 1988.

First published 2008

Printed and bound in the Singapore by Tien Wah Press

Typeset in Swift 9.5 / 13

ISBN 978 1 84471 454 4 hardback

Salt Publishing Ltd gratefully acknowledges
the financial assistance of Arts Council England

1 3 5 7 9 8 6 4 2

For Callum, Kirsty & Cameron

contents

1800

INtRODUCtION

Poetry is an art of navigation, where writers set their minds against the physical and mental landscape of their time and wrestle with their mortal concerns, their needs, hopes and desires. The language of poetry, even at its most transparent, is ambiguous and loaded with meaning, it gives us all access to the dangerous, liberating realm of the imagination, and it allows us to steer away into other lives and other times.

This anthology gives you fifty classic poems which can be repeatedly read, memorized and treasured. Each poet offers you a view from their place in history which will find echoes and reverberations in your own. This is the power of poetry, the only art I know which allows you to hear the heart of the past whilst witnessing our present and imagining our possible futures. In a sense, from out of the past's profound silence, poetry becomes the audible life of the mind. Without it, we would never understand what it is to be human.

In addition, this anthology offers, for the first time, accompanying paintings, photographs and engravings of the very poets themselves—each of them significant artistic works in their own right—so that you can actually *see* who wrote each piece— whose words you are reading right here in these pages.

It strikes me, that looking at poets in this way, seeing their expressions here, their attire and posture captured, is deeply revealing and even mesmerizing—so this is also a book to stare at and wonder.

My chronological selection ranges from Sir Thomas Wyatt through to Rudyard Kipling or, if you prefer, from the early sixteenth century until the beginning of the twentieth. The reader will find sentiments common to us all and it may surprise you to learn you share your thoughts with someone living over four hundred years ago. It never ceases to surprise me how consistent our fears and dreams are throughout history. However, poetry allows us to transcend and transform our own sensibility and the age we live in. It quite literally multiplies the mind and what we may call the landscape of the possible.

I hope you enjoy your encounters here, enough to seek out more work by these poets and their contemporaries—enough to let these writers become part of your own experience, your own navigation system, more intimate and personal than any technology, and ultimately more useful to you, too. With poetry you gain access to the geography of your mind; and there's no limit to that world.

Chris Emery
Great Wilbraham

Tho: Wiatt Knight.

From the Original Drawing by Hans Holbein.   Engrav'd by F. Bartolozzi, R.A. Historical Engraver to his Majesty.

IN HIS MAJESTY'S COLLECTION

Publish'd as the Act directs Oct.r 1.1793. by I. Chamberlaine.

Sir Thomas Wyatt (*c.* 1503–42)
Hans Holbein the Younger

Vixi Puellis Nuper Idoneus . . .

THEY FLEE FROM me that sometime did me seek,
  With naked foot stalking within my chamber:
Once have I seen them gentle, tame, and meek,
    That now are wild, and do not once remember
    That sometime they have put themselves in danger
To take bread at my hand; and now they range,
Busily seeking in continual change.

Thanked be fortune, it hath been otherwise
    Twenty times better; but once especial —
In thin array: after a pleasant guise,
    When her loose gown did from her shoulders fall,
    And she me caught in her arms long and small,
And therewithal so sweetly did me kiss,
And softly said, *'Dear heart, how like you this?'*

It was no dream; for I lay broad awaking:
    But all is turn'd now, through my gentleness,
Into a bitter fashion of forsaking;
    And I have leave to go of her goodness;
    And she also to use new-fangleness.
But since that I unkindly so am servèd,
'How like you this?' — what hath she now deservèd?

SIR THOMAS WYATT

Edmund Spenser (*c*.1552–99)
Henry Bone

Whilst it is Prime

FRESH SPRING, THE herald of loves mighty king,
In whose cote-armour richly are displayed
All sorts of flowers, the which on earth do spring,
In goodly colours gloriously arrayd —
Goe to my love, where she is carelesse layd,
Yet in her winters bowre not well awake;
Tell her the joyous time will not be staid,
Unlesse she doe him by the forelock take;
Bid her therefore her selfe soone ready make,
To wayt on Love amongst his lovely crew;
Where every one, that misseth then her make,
Shall be by him amearst with penance dew.
    Make hast, therefore, sweet love, whilest it is prime;
    For none can call againe the passèd time.

EDMUND SPENSER

Fulke Greville, Lord Brooke (1554–1628)
English School 19th century

Myra

I, WITH WHOSE colours Myra dress'd her head,
   I, that ware posies of her own hand-making,
I, that mine own name in the chimneys read
   By Myra finely wrought ere I was waking:
Must I look on, in hope time coming may
With change bring back my turn again to play?

I, that on Sunday at the church-stile found
   A garland sweet with true-love-knots in flowers,
Which I to wear about mine arms was bound
   That each of us might know that all was ours:
Must I lead now an idle life in wishes,
And follow Cupid for his loaves and fishes?

I, that did wear the ring her mother left,
   I, for whose love she gloried to be blamed,
I, with whose eyes her eyes committed theft,
   I, who did make her blush when I was named:
Must I lose ring, flowers, blush, theft, and go naked,
Watching with sighs till dead love be awaked?

Was it for this that I might Myra see
   Washing the water with her beauty's white?
Yet would she never write her love to me.
   Thinks wit of change when thoughts are in delight?
Mad girls may safely love as they may leave;
No man can *print* a kiss: lines may deceive.

FULKE GREVILLE, LORD BROOKE

William Shakespeare (1564–1616)
Martin Droeshout

Fidele

FEAR NO MORE the heat o' the sun,
　　Nor the furious winter's rages;
Thou thy worldly task hast done,
　　Home art done, and ta'en thy wages:
Golden lads and girls all must,
As chimney-sweepers, come to dust.

Fear no more the frown o' the great;
　　Thou art past the tyrant's stroke;
Care no more to clothe and eat;
　　To thee the reed is as the oak:
The Sceptre, Learning, Physic, must
All follow this, and come to dust.

Fear no more the lightning-flash,
　　Nor the all-dreaded thunder-stone;
Fear not slander, censure rash;
　　Thou hast finished joy and moan:
All lovers young, all lovers must
Consign to thee, and come to dust.

No exorciser harm thee!
Nor no witchcraft charm thee!
Ghost unlaid forbear thee!
Nothing ill come near thee!
Quiet consummation have,
And renownèd by thy grave!

WILLIAM SHAKESPEARE

9

Ben Jonson (1572–1637)
Gerrit van Honthorst

The Ecstasy

WHERE, LIKE A pillow on a bed,
    A pregnant bank swell'd up, to rest
The violet's reclining head,
    Sat we two, one another's best.

Our hands were firmly cèmented
    By a fast balm which thence did spring;
Our eye-beams twisted, and did thread
    Our eyes upon one double string.

So to engraft our hands, as yet
    Was all the means to make us one;
And pictures in our eyes to get
    Was all our propagation.

As 'twixt two equal armies Fate
    Suspends uncertain victory,
Our souls—which to advance their state
    Were gone out—hung 'twixt her and me.

And whilst our souls negotiate there,
    We like sepulchral statues lay;
All day the same our postures were,
    And we said nothing, all the day.

JOHN DONNE

William Drummond (1585–1649)
Scottish School 17th century

Change Should Breed Change

NEW DOTH THE sun appear,
  The mountains' snows decay,
Crown'd with frail flowers forth comes the baby year.
    My soul, time posts away;
    And thou yet in that frost
    Which flower and fruit hath lost,
As if all here immortal were, dost stay.
    For shame! thy powers awake,
Look to that Heaven which never night makes black,
And there at that immortal sun's bright rays,
Deck thee with flowers which fear not rage of days!

WILLIAM DRUMMOND

Robert Herrick (1591–1674)
William Marshall

To the Virgins, to Make Much of Time

GATHER YE ROSEBUDS while ye may,
  Old Time is still a-flying:
And this same flower that smiles to-day
    To-morrow will be dying.

The glorious lamp of heaven, the sun,
    The higher he's a-getting,
The sooner will his race be run,
    And nearer he's to setting.

That age is best which is the first,
    When youth and blood are warmer;
But being spent, the worse, and worst
    Times still succeed the former.

Then be not coy, but use your time,
    And while ye may, go marry:
For having lost but once your prime,
    You may for ever tarry.

ROBERT HERRICK

The Effigies of Mr George Herbert:
Author of those Sacred Poems called
The Temple.

George Herbert (1593–1633)
English School 17th century

Virtue

SWEET DAY, so cool, so calm, so bright!
The bridal of the earth and sky—
The dew shall weep thy fall to-night;
    For thou must die.

Sweet rose, whose hue angry and brave
Bids the rash gazer wipe his eye,
Thy root is ever in its grave,
    And thou must die.

Sweet spring, full of sweet days and roses,
A box where sweets compacted lie,
My music shows ye have your closes,
    And all must die.

Only a sweet and virtuous soul,
Like season'd timber, never gives;
But though the whole world turn to coal,
    Then chiefly lives.

GEORGE HERBERT

Sir William Davenant (1606–68)
English School 17th century

Aubade

THE LARK NOW leaves his wat'ry nest,
  And climbing shakes his dewy wings.
He takes this window for the East,
  And to implore your light he sings—
Awake, awake! the morn will never rise
Till she can dress her beauty at your eyes.

The merchant bows unto the seaman's star,
  The ploughman from the sun his season takes,
But still the lover wonders what they are
  Who look for day before his mistress wakes.
Awake, awake! break thro' your veils of lawn!
Then draw your curtains, and begin the dawn!

                    SIR WILLIAM DAVENANT

John Milton (1608–74)
English School 18th century

On His Deceased Wife

METHOUGHT I SAW my late espousèd Saint
Brought to me like Alcestis from the grave,
  Whom Joves great Son to her glad Husband gave,
  Rescu'd from death by force though pale and faint.
Mine as whom washt from spot of child-bed taint,
  Purification in the old Law did save,
  And such, as yet once more I trust to have
  Full sight of her in Heaven without restraint,
Came vested all in white, pure as her mind:
  Her face was vail'd, yet to my fancied sight,
  Love, sweetness, goodness, in her person shin'd
So clear, as in no face with more delight.
  But O as to embrace me she enclin'd
  I wak'd, she fled, and day brought back my night.

JOHN MILTON

ANDREW MARVELL.

To Hugh Bethell Esq.ʳ of Rise in Holderness, This Portrait of his celebrated & patriotic Ancestor is Dedicated by his most obedᵗ Servant.

Andrew Marvell (1621–1678)
English School 17th century

Bermudas

WHERE THE REMOTE Bermudas ride
  In the ocean's bosom unespied,
From a small boat that row'd along
The listening woods received this song:
  'What should we do but sing His praise
That led us through the watery maze
Unto an isle so long unknown,
And yet far kinder than our own?
Where He the huge sea-monsters wracks,
That lift the deep upon their backs,
He lands us on a grassy stage,
Safe from the storms' and prelates' rage:
He gave us this eternal Spring
Which here enamels everything,
And sends the fowls to us in care
On daily visits through the air:
He hangs in shades the orange bright
Like golden lamps in a green night,
And does in the pomegranates close
Jewels more rich than Ormus shows:
He makes the figs our mouths to meet
And throws the melons at our feet;
But apples plants of such a price,
No tree could ever bear them twice.
With cedars chosen by His hand
From Lebanon He stores the land;
And makes the hollow seas that roar
Proclaim the ambergris on shore.
He cast (of which we rather boast)
The Gospel's pearl upon our coast;
And in these rocks for us did frame
A temple where to sound His name.
O, let our voice His praise exalt
Till it arrive at Heaven's vault,
Which thence (perhaps) rebounding may
Echo beyond the Mexique bay!'

Thus sung they in the English boat
A holy and a cheerful note:
And all the way, to guide their chime,
With falling oars they kept the time.

ANDREW MARVELL

25

Margaret Cavendish, Duchess of Newcastle (1624–74)
English School 17th century

A World Made by Atoms

SMALL ATOMS OF themselves a world may make,
For being subtle, every shape they take;
And as they dance about, they places find,
Of forms, that best agree, make every kind.
For when we build an house of brick, or stone,
We lay them even, every one by one:
And when we find a gap that's big, or small,
We seek out stones to fit that place withal.
For when as they too big, or little be,
They fall away, and cannot stay, we see.
So atoms, as they dance, find places fit,
And there remaining close and fast will knit.
Those which not fit, the rest that rove about,
Do never leave, until they thrust them out.
Thus by their forms and motions they will be,
Like workmen, which amongst themselves agree;
And so, by chance, may a new world create:
Or else predestinate, may work by fate.

MARGARET CAVENDISH

John Dryden (1631–1700)

Johann Closterman

Hidden Flame

I FEED A flame within, which so torments me
That it both pains my heart, and yet contents me:
'Tis such a pleasing smart, and I so love it,
That I had rather die than once remove it.

Yet he, for whom I grieve, shall never know it;
My tongue does not betray, nor my eyes show it.
Not a sigh, nor a tear, my pain discloses,
But they fall silently, like dew on roses.

Thus, to prevent my Love from being cruel,
My heart's the sacrifice, as 'tis the fuel;
And while I suffer this to give him quiet,
My faith rewards my love, though he deny it.

On his eyes will I gaze, and there delight me;
While I conceal my love no frown can fright me.
To be more happy I dare not aspire,
Nor can I fall more low, mounting no higher.

JOHN DRYDEN

Aphra Behn (1640–89)
Sir Peter Lely

The Libertine

A THOUSAND MARTYRS I have made,
   All sacrificed to my desire,
A thousand beauties have betray'd
   That languish in resistless fire:
The untamed heart to hand I brought,
And fix'd the wild and wand'ring thought.

I never vow'd nor sigh'd in vain,
   But both, tho' false, were well received;
The fair are pleased to give us pain,
   And what they wish is soon believed:
And tho' I talk'd of wounds and smart,
Love's pleasures only touch'd my heart.

Alone the glory and the spoil
   I always laughing bore away;
The triumphs without pain or toil,
   Without the hell the heaven of joy;
And while I thus at random rove
Despise the fools that whine for love.

ApHRA BEHN

John Wilmot, Earl of Rochester (1647–80)
Jacob Huysmans

Return

Absent from thee, I languish still;
  Then ask me not, When I return?
The straying fool 'twill plainly kill
  To wish all day, all night to mourn.

Dear, from thine arms then let me fly,
  That my fantastic mind may prove
The torments it deserves to try,
  That tears my fix'd heart from my love.

When, wearied with a world of woe,
  To thy safe bosom I retire,
Where love, and peace, and truth does flow,
  May I contented there expire!

Lest, once more wandering from that heaven,
  I fall on some base heart unblest;
Faithless to thee, false, unforgiven—
  And lose my everlasting rest.

JOHN WILMOT, EARL OF ROCHESTER

Anne Wharton (1659–85)
English School 19th century

Song

How hardly I conceal'd my tears?
  How oft did I complain?
When, many tedious days, my fears
    Told me I lov'd in vain.

But now my joys as wild are grown,
    And hard to be concealed;
Sorrow may make a silent moan,
    But joy will be reveal'd.

I tell it to the bleating flocks,
    To every stream and tree;
And bless the hollow murm'ring rocks
    For echoing back to me.

Thus you may see with how much joy
    We want, we wish, believe;
'Tis hard such passion to destroy,
    But easy to deceive.

ANNE WHARTON

William Congreve (1670–1729)
Sir Godfrey Kneller engraved by John Faber

A Hue and Cry After Fair Amoret

Fair Amoret is gone astray—
    Pursue and seek her, ev'ry lover;
I'll tell the signs by which you may
    The wand'ring Shepherdess discover.

Coquette and coy at once her air,
    Both studied, tho' both seem neglected;
Careless she is, with artful care,
    Affecting to seem unaffected.

With skill her eyes dart ev'ry glance,
    Yet change so soon you'd ne'er suspect them,
For she'd persuade they wound by chance,
    Tho' certain aim and art direct them.

She likes herself, yet others hates
    For that which in herself she prizes;
And, while she laughs at them, forgets
    She is the thing that she despises.

WILLIAM CONGREVE

John Gay (1685–1732)
Jonathan Richardson

Song

O RUDDIER THAN the cherry!
O sweeter than the berry!
  O nymph more bright
  Than moonshine night,
Like kidlings blithe and merry!
Ripe as the melting cluster!
No lily has such lustre;
    Yet hard to tame
    As raging flame,
And fierce as storms that bluster!

JOHN GAY

Alexander Pope (1688–1744)
Jonathan Richardson

The Dying Christian to his Soul

VITAL SPARK OF heav'nly flame!
   Quit, O quit this mortal frame:
Trembling, hoping, ling'ring, flying,
   O the pain, the bliss of dying!
Cease, fond Nature, cease thy strife,
And let me languish into life.

   Hark! they whisper; angels say,
   Sister Spirit, come away!
   What is this absorbs me quite?
   Steals my senses, shuts my sight,
Drowns my spirits, draws my breath?
Tell me, my soul, can this be death?

The world recedes; it disappears!
Heav'n opens on my eyes! my ears
   With sounds seraphic ring!
Lend, lend your wings! I mount! I fly!
O Grave! where is thy victory?
   O Death! where is thy sting?

ALEXANDER POPE

Lady Mary Wortley Montagu (1689–1762)
Sir Godfrey Kneller

The Politicians

IN ANCIENT DAYS when every brute
To humble privilege had right;
Could reason, wrangle, or dispute,
    As well as scratch, and tear, and bite;

When Phoebus shone his brightest ray,
    The rip'ning corn his pow'r confessed;
His cheering beams made Nature gay,
    The eagle in his warmth was blest.

But malcontents e'en then arose,
    The birds who love the dolesome night
The darkest grove with care they chose,
    And there caball'd against the light.

The screech-owl, with ill-boding cry,
    Portends strange things, old women say,
Stops ev'ry fool that passes by,
    And frights the schoolboy from his play.

The raven and the double bat,
    With families of owls combine;
In close consult they rail and chat,
    And curse aloud the glorious shine.

While the great planet, all serene,
    Heedless pursues his destin'd way,
He asks not what these murmurs mean,
    But runs his course, and gives us day.

LADY MARY WORTLEY MONTAGU

Dr. Samuel Johnson (1709–84)
Sir Joshua Reynolds

To Sir John Lade, on His Coming of Age
'A Short Song of Congratulation'

LONG-EXPECTED ONE-and-twenty,
   Ling'ring year, at length is flown:
Pride and pleasure, pomp and plenty,
   Great Sir John, are now your own.

Loosen'd from the minor's tether,
   Free to mortgage or to sell,
Wild as wind, and light as feather,
   Bid the sons of thrift farewell.

Call the Betsies, Kates, and Jennies,
   All the names that banish care;
Lavish of your grandsire's guineas,
   Show the spirit of an heir.

All that prey on vice and folly
   Joy to see their quarry fly:
There the gamester, light and jolly,
   There the lender, grave and sly.

Wealth, Sir John, was made to wander,
   Let it wander as it will;
Call the jockey, call the pander,
   Bid them come and take their fill.

When the bonny blade carouses,
   Pockets full, and spirits high—
What are acres? What are houses?
   Only dirt, or wet or dry.

Should the guardian friend or mother
   Tell the woes of wilful waste,
Scorn their counsel, scorn their pother;—
   You can hang or drown at last!

DR. SAMUEL JOHNSON

Thomas Gray (1716–71)
Arthur Pond

On a Favourite Cat, Drowned in a Tub of Gold Fishes

T WAS ON A lofty vase's side,
　Where China's gayest art had dyed
　　The azure flowers that blow;
Demurest of the tabby kind,
The pensive Selima reclined,
　　Gazed on the lake below.

Her conscious tail her joy declared;
The fair round face, the snowy beard,
　　The velvet of her paws,
Her coat, that with the tortoise vies,
Her ears of jet, and emerald eyes,
　　She saw; and purr'd applause.

Still had she gazed; but 'midst the tide
Two angel forms were seen to glide,
　　The Genii of the stream:
Their scaly armour's Tyrian hue
Thro' richest purple to the view
　　Betray'd a golden gleam.

The hapless Nymph with wonder saw:
A whisker first and then a claw,
　　With many an ardent wish,
She stretch'd in vain to reach the prize.
What female heart can gold despise?
　　What Cat's averse to fish?

Presumptuous Maid! with looks intent
Again she stretch'd, again she bent,
　　Nor knew the gulf between.
(Malignant Fate sat by, and smiled.)
The slipp'ry verge her feet beguiled,
　　She tumbled headlong in.

Eight times emerging from the flood
She mew'd to ev'ry wat'ry god,
　　Some speedy aid to send.
No Dolphin came, no Nereid stirr'd:
Nor cruel *Tom*, nor *Susan* heard.
　　A Fav'rite has no friend!

From hence, ye Beauties, undeceived,
Know, one false step is ne'er retrieved,
　　And be with caution bold.
Not all that tempts your wand'ring eyes
And heedless hearts, is lawful prize;
　　Nor all that glisters, gold.

THOMAS GRAY

OLIVER GOLDSMITH.

Oliver Goldsmith (1730–74)
English School 19th century

Woman

WHEN LOVELY WOMAN stoops to folly,
  And finds too late that men betray,
What charm can soothe her melancholy?
  What art can wash her tears away?

The only art her guilt to cover,
  To hide her shame from ev'ry eye,
To give repentance to her lover,
  And wring his bosom is—to die.

OLIVER GOLDSMITH

William Cowper (1731–1800)
William Blake

To Mary Unwin

MARY! I WANT a lyre with other strings,
  Such aid from Heaven as some have feign'd they drew,
An eloquence scarce given to mortals, new
And undebased by praise of meaner things;
That ere through age or woe I shed my wings,
I may record thy worth with honour due,
In verse as musical as thou art true,
And that immortalizes whom it sings:
But thou hast little need. There is a Book
By seraphs writ with beams of heavenly light,
On which the eyes of God not rarely look,
A chronicle of actions just and bright —
    There all thy deeds, my faithful Mary, shine;
    And since thou own'st that praise, I spare thee mine.

WILLIAM COWPER

William Blake (1757–1827)

John Linnell

Hear the Voice

HEAR THE VOICE of the Bard,
Who present, past, and future, sees;
Whose ears have heard
The Holy Word
That walk'd among the ancient trees;

Calling the lapsèd soul,
And weeping in the evening dew;
That might control
The starry pole,
And fallen, fallen light renew!

'O Earth, O Earth, return!
Arise from out the dewy grass!
Night is worn,
And the morn
Rises from the slumbrous mass.

'Turn away no more;
Why wilt thou turn away?
The starry floor,
The watery shore,
Is given thee till the break of day.'

WILLIAM BLAKE

Robert Burns (1759–96)
Alexander Nasmyth

A Red, Red Rose

O MY LUVE's like a red, red rose
   That's newly sprung in June:
O my Luve's like the melodie
   That's sweetly play'd in tune!

As fair art thou, my bonnie lass,
   So deep in luve am I:
And I will luve thee still, my dear,
   Till a' the seas gang dry:

Till a' the seas gang dry, my dear,
   And the rocks melt wi' the sun;
I will luve thee still, my dear,
   While the sands o' life shall run.

And fare thee weel, my only Luve,
   And fare thee weel a while!
And I will come again, my Luve,
   Tho' it were ten thousand mile.

ROBERT BURNS

Mary Ann Lamb (1764–1867)
English School 19th century

A Child

A CHILD'S A plaything for an hour;
  Its pretty tricks we try
For that or for a longer space—
  Then tire, and lay it by.

But I knew one that to itself
  All seasons could control;
That would have mock'd the sense of pain
  Out of a grievèd soul.

Thou straggler into loving arms,
  Young climber-up of knees,
When I forget thy thousand ways
  Then life and all shall cease.

MARY ANN LAMB

William Wordsworth (1770–1850)
Benjamin Robert Haydon

The World

THE WORLD IS too much with us; late and soon,
Getting and spending, we lay waste our powers:
   Little we see in Nature that is ours;
We have given our hearts away, a sordid boon!
This sea that bares her bosom to the moon;
   The winds that will be howling at all hours,
   And are up-gather'd now like sleeping flowers;
For this, for everything, we are out of tune;
It moves us not.—Great God! I'd rather be
   A Pagan suckled in a creed outworn;
So might I, standing on this pleasant lea,
   Have glimpses that would make me less forlorn;
Have sight of Proteus rising from the sea;
   Or hear old Triton blow his wreathèd horn.

WILLIAM WORDSWORTH

Sir Walter Scott (1771–1832)
Sir Francis Grant

Patriotism

1. INNOMINATUS

BREATHES THERE THE man with soul so dead,
Who never to himself hath said,
   'This is my own, my native land!'
Whose heart hath ne'er within him burn'd
As home his footsteps he hath turn'd
   From wandering on a foreign strand?
If such there breathe, go, mark him well;
For him no Minstrel raptures swell;
High though his titles, proud his name,
Boundless his wealth as wish can claim;
Despite those titles, power, and pelf,
The wretch, concentred all in self,
Living, shall forfeit fair renown,
And, doubly dying, shall go down
To the vile dust from whence he sprung,
Unwept, unhonour'd, and unsung.

SIR WALTER SCOTT

Samuel Taylor Coleridge (1772–1834)
James Northcote

Work Without Hope

ALL NATURE SEEMS at work. Slugs leave their lair—
The bees are stirring—birds are on the wing—
And Winter, slumbering in the open air,
Wears on his smiling face a dream of Spring!
And I, the while, the sole unbusy thing,
Nor honey make, nor pair, nor build, nor sing.

Yet well I ken the banks where amaranths blow,
Have traced the fount whence streams of nectar flow.
Bloom, O ye amaranths! bloom for whom ye may,
For me ye bloom not! Glide, rich streams, away!
With lips unbrighten'd, wreathless brow, I stroll:
And would you learn the spells that drowse my soul?
Work without Hope draws nectar in a sieve,
And Hope without an object cannot live.

SAMUEL TAYLOR COLERIDGE

Charles Lamb (1775–1834)
English School 17th century

The Old Familiar Faces

I HAVE HAD playmates, I have had companions,
In my days of childhood, in my joyful school-days —
All, all are gone, the old familiar faces.

I have been laughing, I have been carousing,
Drinking late, sitting late, with my bosom cronies —
All, all are gone, the old familiar faces.

I loved a Love once, fairest among women:
Closed are her doors on me, I must not see her —
All, all are gone, the old familiar faces.

I have a friend, a kinder friend has no man:
Like an ingrate, I left my friend abruptly;
Left him, to muse on the old familiar faces.

Ghost-like I paced round the haunts of my childhood,
Earth seem'd a desert I was bound to traverse,
Seeking to find the old familiar faces.

Friend of my bosom, thou more than a brother,
Why wert not thou born in my father's dwelling?
So might we talk of the old familiar faces —

How some they have died, and some they have left me,
And some are taken from me; all are departed —
All, all are gone, the old familiar faces.

CHARLES LAMB

Mary Robinson (1783–84)
Sir Joshua Reynolds

January 1795

PAVEMENT SLIPP'RY, PEOPLE sneezing,
Lords in ermine, beggars freezing;
Titled gluttons dainties carving,
Genius in a garret starving.

Lofty mansions, warm and spacious;
Courtiers cringing and voracious;
Misers scarce and wretched heeding;
Gallant soldiers fighting, bleeding.

Wives who laugh at passive spouses;
Theatres, and meeting-houses;
Balls, where simp'ring misses languish;
Hospitals, and groans of anguish.

Arts and sciences bewailing:
Commerce drooping, credit failing:
Placemen mocking subjects loyal;
Separations, weddings royal.

Authors who can't earn a dinner;
Many a subtle rogue a winner;
Fugitives for shelter seeking;
Misers hoarding, tradesmen breaking.

Taste and talents quite deserted;
All the laws of truth perverted;
Arrogance o'er merit soaring;
Merit silently deploring.

Ladies gambling night and morning;
Fools the works of genius scorning;
Ancient dames for girls mistaken;
Youthful damsels quite forsaken.

Some in luxury delighting;
More in talking than in fighting;
Lovers old, and beaux decrepid;
Lordlings empty and insipid.

Poets, painters, and musicians;
Lawyers, doctors, politicians;
Pamphlets, newspapers, and odes
Seeking fame by different roads.

Gallant souls with empty purses;
Gen'rals only fit for nurses;
School-boys, smit with martial spirit,
Taking place of vet'ran merit.

Honest men who can't get places,
Knaves who show unblushing faces:
Ruin hasten'd, peace retarded;
Candour spurn'd, and art rewarded.

MARY ROBINSON

Thomas Love Peacock (1785–1866)
English Photographer 19th century

The Grave of Love

I DUG, BENEATH the cypress shade,
  What well might seem an elfin's grave;
And every pledge in earth I laid,
  That erst thy false affection gave.

I press'd them down the sod beneath;
  I placed one mossy stone above;
And twined the rose's fading wreath
  Around the sepulchre of love.

Frail as thy love, the flowers were dead
  Ere yet the evening sun was set:
But years shall see the cypress spread,
  Immutable as my regret.

THOMAS LOVE PEACOCK

Lord George Gordon Byron (1788–1824)
Thomas Phillips

When We Two Parted

WHEN WE TWO parted
   In silence and tears,
Half broken-hearted
   To sever for years,
Pale grew thy cheek and cold,
  Colder thy kiss;
Truly that hour foretold
   Sorrow to this.

The dew of the morning
   Sunk chill on my brow—
It felt like the warning
   Of what I feel now.
Thy vows are all broken,
   And light is thy fame:
I hear thy name spoken,
   And share in its shame.

They name thee before me,
   A knell to mine ear;
A shudder comes o'er me—
   Why wert thou so dear?
They know not I knew thee,
   Who knew thee too well:
Long, long shall I rue thee,
   Too deeply to tell.

In secret we met—
   In silence I grieve,
That thy heart could forget,
   Thy spirit deceive.
If I should meet thee
   After long years,
How should I greet thee?
   With silence and tears.

LORD GEORGE GORDON BYRON

Percy Bysshe Shelley (1792–1822)
Amelia Curran

Remorse

AWAY! THE MOOR is dark beneath the moon,
  Rapid clouds have drunk the last pale beam of even:
Away! the gathering winds will call the darkness soon,
  And profoundest midnight shroud the serene lights of heaven.
Pause not! the time is past! Every voice cries, 'Away!'
  Tempt not with one last tear thy friend's ungentle mood:
Thy lover's eye, so glazed and cold, dares not entreat thy stay:
  Duty and dereliction guide thee back to solitude.

Away, away! to thy sad and silent home;
  Pour bitter tears on its desolated hearth;
Watch the dim shades as like ghosts they go and come,
  And complicate strange webs of melancholy mirth.
The leaves of wasted autumn woods shall float around thine head,
  The blooms of dewy Spring shall gleam beneath thy feet:
But thy soul or this world must fade in the frost that binds the dead,
  Ere midnight's frown and morning's smile, ere thou and peace, may meet.

The cloud shadows of midnight possess their own repose,
  For the weary winds are silent, or the moon is in the deep;
Some respite to its turbulence unresting ocean knows;
  Whatever moves or toils or grieves hath its appointed sleep.
Thou in the grave shalt rest:—yet, till the phantoms flee,
  Which that house and heath and garden made dear to thee erewhile,
Thy remembrance and repentance and deep musings are not free
  From the music of two voices, and the light of one sweet smile.

PERCY BYSSHE SHELLEY

John Clare (1793–1864)
Samuel Freeman

Written in Northampton County Asylum

I AM! YET what I am who cares, or knows?
   My friends forsake me like a memory lost.
I am the self-consumer of my woes;
   They rise and vanish, an oblivious host,
Shadows of life, whose very soul is lost.
And yet I am—I live—though I am toss'd

Into the nothingness of scorn and noise,
   Into the living sea of waking dream,
Where there is neither sense of life, nor joys,
   But the huge shipwreck of my own esteem
And all that's dear. Even those I loved the best
Are strange—nay, they are stranger than the rest.

I long for scenes where man has never trod—
   For scenes where woman never smiled or wept—
There to abide with my Creator, God,
   And sleep as I in childhood sweetly slept,
Full of high thoughts, unborn. So let me lie,—
The grass below; above, the vaulted sky.

JOHN CLARE

John Keats (1795–1821)
Joseph Severn

Ode on Melancholy

No, no! go not to Lethe, neither twist
　　Wolf's-bane, tight-rooted, for its poisonous wine;
Nor suffer thy pale forehead to be kist
　　By nightshade, ruby grape of Proserpine;
Make not your rosary of yew-berries,
　　Nor let the beetle, nor the death-moth be
　　　Your mournful Psyche, nor the downy owl
A partner in your sorrow's mysteries;
　　For shade to shade will come too drowsily,
　　　And drown the wakeful anguish of the soul.

But when the melancholy fit shall fall
　　Sudden from heaven like a weeping cloud,
That fosters the droop-headed flowers all,
　　And hides the green hill in an April shroud;
Then glut thy sorrow on a morning rose,
　　Or on the rainbow of the salt sand-wave,
　　　Or on the wealth of globèd peonies;
Or if thy mistress some rich anger shows,
　　Emprison her soft hand, and let her rave,
　　　And feed deep, deep upon her peerless eyes.

She dwells with Beauty—Beauty that must die;
　　And Joy, whose hand is ever at his lips
Bidding adieu; and aching Pleasure nigh,
　　Turning to poison while the bee-mouth sips:
Ay, in the very temple of Delight
　　Veil'd Melancholy has her sovran shrine,
　　　Though seen of none save him whose strenuous tongue
Can burst Joy's grape against his palate fine;
　　His soul shall taste the sadness of her might,
　　　And be among her cloudy trophies hung.

JOHN KEATS

Elizabeth Barrett Browning (1806–61)
English School 19th century

Grief

I TELL YOU, hopeless grief is passionless;
  That only men incredulous of despair,
    Half-taught in anguish, through the midnight air
Beat upward to God's throne in loud access
Of shrieking and reproach. Full desertness
    In souls as countries lieth silent-bare
    Under the blanching, vertical eye-glare
Of the absolute Heavens. Deep-hearted man, express
Grief for thy Dead in silence like to death—
    Most like a monumental statue set
In everlasting watch and moveless woe
Till itself crumble to the dust beneath.
    Touch it; the marble eyelids are not wet:
If it could weep, it could arise and go.

ELIZABETH BARRETT BROWNING

Lord Alfred Tennyson (1809–92)
Alice Hambidge

Come Down, O Maid

COME DOWN, O maid, from yonder mountain height:
What pleasure lives in height (the shepherd sang),
In height and cold, the splendour of the hills?
But cease to move so near the Heavens, and cease
To glide a sunbeam by the blasted Pine,
To sit a star upon the sparkling spire;
And come, for Love is of the valley, come,
For Love is of the valley, come thou down
And find him; by the happy threshold, he,
Or hand in hand with Plenty in the maize,
Or red with spirted purple of the vats,
Or foxlike in the vine; nor cares to walk
With Death and Morning on the silver horns,
Nor wilt thou snare him in the white ravine,
Nor find him dropt upon the firths of ice,
That huddling slant in furrow-cloven falls
To roll the torrent out of dusky doors:
But follow; let the torrent dance thee down
To find him in the valley; let the wild
Lean-headed Eagles yelp alone, and leave
The monstrous ledges there to slope, and spill
Their thousand wreaths of dangling water-smoke,
That like a broken purpose waste in air:
So waste not thou; but come; for all the vales
Await thee; azure pillars of the hearth
Arise to thee; the children call, and I
Thy shepherd pipe, and sweet is every sound,
Sweeter thy voice, but every sound is sweet;
Myriads of rivulets hurrying thro' the lawn,
The moan of doves in immemorial elms,
And murmuring of innumerable bees.

LORD ALFRED TENNYSON

Robert Browning (1812–89)
Dante Gabriel Rossetti

Home-thoughts, from Abroad

O TO BE in England
Now that April's there,
And whoever wakes in England
Sees, some morning, unaware,
That the lowest boughs and the brushwood sheaf
Round the elm-tree bole are in tiny leaf,
While the chaffinch sings on the orchard bough
In England—now!

And after April, when May follows,
And the whitethroat builds, and all the swallows!
Hark, where my blossom'd pear-tree in the hedge
Leans to the field and scatters on the clover
Blossoms and dewdrops—at the bent spray's edge—
That 's the wise thrush; he sings each song twice over,
Lest you should think he never could recapture
The first fine careless rapture!
And though the fields look rough with hoary dew,
All will be gay when noontide wakes anew
The buttercups, the little children's dower
—Far brighter than this gaudy melon-flower!

ROBERT BROWNING

Emily Brontë
from a painting of a family group by Branwell Brontë.

Published by Harper & Brothers, New York.

Emily Brontë (1818–48)
Patrick Branwell Brontë

Remembrance

COLD IN THE earth—and the deep snow piled above thee,
　　Far, far removed, cold in the dreary grave!
Have I forgot, my only Love, to love thee,
　　Sever'd at last by Time's all-severing wave?

Now, when alone, do my thoughts no longer hover
　　Over the mountains, on that northern shore,
Resting their wings where heath and fern-leaves cover
　　Thy noble heart for ever, ever more?

Cold in the earth—and fifteen wild Decembers
　　From those brown hills have melted into spring:
Faithful, indeed, is the spirit that remembers
　　After such years of change and suffering!

Sweet Love of youth, forgive, if I forget thee,
　　While the world's tide is bearing me along;
Other desires and other hopes beset me,
　　Hopes which obscure, but cannot do thee wrong!

No later light has lighten'd up my heaven,
　　No second morn has ever shone for me;
All my life's bliss from thy dear life was given,
　　All my life's bliss is in the grave with thee.

But when the days of golden dreams had perish'd,
　　And even Despair was powerless to destroy;
Then did I learn how existence could be cherish'd,
　　Strengthen'd and fed without the aid of joy.

Then did I check the tears of useless passion—
　　Wean'd my young soul from yearning after thine;
Sternly denied its burning wish to hasten
　　Down to that tomb already more than mine.

And, even yet, I dare not let it languish,
　　Dare not indulge in memory's rapturous pain;
Once drinking deep of that divinest anguish,
　　How could I seek the empty world again?　　EMILY BRONTË

Matthew Arnold (1822–88)
English School 19th century

To Marguerite

Yes: in the sea of life enisled,
   With echoing straits between us thrown.
Dotting the shoreless watery wild,
   We mortal millions live *alone*.
The islands feel the enclasping flow,
And then their endless bounds they know.

But when the moon their hollows lights,
   And they are swept by balms of spring,
And in their glens, on starry nights,
   The nightingales divinely sing;
And lovely notes, from shore to shore,
Across the sounds and channels pour;

O then a longing like despair
   Is to their farthest caverns sent!
For surely once, they feel, we were
   Parts of a single continent.
Now round us spreads the watery plain—
O might our marges meet again!

Who order'd that their longing's fire
   Should be, as soon as kindled, cool'd?
Who renders vain their deep desire?—
   A God, a God their severance ruled;
And bade betwixt their shores to be
The unplumb'd, salt, estranging sea.

Matthew Arnold

George Meredith (1828–1909)
English School 19th century

Lucifer in Starlight

ON A STARR'D night Prince Lucifer uprose.
  Tired of his dark dominion swung the fiend
  Above the rolling ball in cloud part screen'd,
Where sinners hugg'd their spectre of repose.
Poor prey to his hot fit of pride were those.
  And now upon his western wing he lean'd,
  Now his huge bulk o'er Afric's sands careen'd,
Now the black planet shadow'd Arctic snows.
Soaring through wider zones that prick'd his scars
  With memory of the old revolt from Awe,
He reach'd a middle height, and at the stars,
Which are the brain of heaven, he look'd, and sank.
Around the ancient track march'd, rank on rank,
  The army of unalterable law.

GEORGE MEREDITH

Christina Rossetti (1830–94)
Dante Gabriel Rossetti

A Birthday

MY HEART IS like a singing bird
　　Whose nest is in a water'd shoot;
My heart is like an apple-tree
　　Whose boughs are bent with thick-set fruit;
My heart is like a rainbow shell
　　That paddles in a halcyon sea;
My heart is gladder than all these,
　　Because my love is come to me.

Raise me a daïs of silk and down;
　　Hang it with vair and purple dyes;
Carve it in doves and pomegranates,
　　And peacocks with a hundred eyes;
Work it in gold and silver grapes,
　　In leaves and silver fleurs-de-lys;
Because the birthday of my life
　　Is come, my love is come to me.

CHRISTINA ROSSETTI

Algernon Charles Swinburne (1837–1909)
William Bell Scott

Love and Sleep

LYING ASLEEP BETWEEN the strokes of night
I saw my love lean over my sad bed,
Pale as the duskiest lily's leaf or head,
Smooth-skinned and dark, with bare throat made to bite,
Too wan for blushing and too warm for white,
But perfect-coloured without white or red.
And her lips opened amorously, and said —
I wist not what, saving one word — Delight
And all her face was honey to my mouth,
And all her body pasture to mine eyes;
The long lithe arms and hotter hands than fire,
The quivering flanks, hair smelling of the south,
The bright light feet, the splendid supple thighs
And glittering eyelids of my soul's desire.

ALGERNON CHARLES SWINBURNE

Robert Bridges (1844–1930)
English School 20th century

A Passer-by

WHITHER, O SPLENDID ship, thy white sails crowding,
    Leaning across the bosom of the urgent West,
That fearest nor sea rising, nor sky clouding,
    Whither away, fair rover, and what thy quest?
    Ah! soon, when Winter has all our vales opprest,
When skies are cold and misty, and hail is hurling,
    Wilt thoù glìde on the blue Pacific, or rest
In a summer haven asleep, thy white sails furling.

I there before thee, in the country that well thou knowest,
    Already arrived am inhaling the odorous air:
I watch thee enter unerringly where thou goest,
    And anchor queen of the strange shipping there,
    Thy sails for awnings spread, thy masts bare:
Nor is aught from the foaming reef to the snow-capp'd grandest
    Peak, that is over the feathery palms, more fair
Than thou, so upright, so stately and still thou standest.

And yet, O splendid ship, unhail'd and nameless,
    I know not if, aiming a fancy, I rightly divine
That thou hast a purpose joyful, a courage blameless,
    Thy port assured in a happier land than mine.
    But for all I have given thee, beauty enough is thine,
As thou, aslant with trim tackle and shrouding,
    From the proud nostril curve of a prow's line
In the offing scatterest foam, thy white sails crowding.

ROBERT BRIDGES

Robert Louis Stevenson (1850–94)
Sir William Blake Richmond

Romance

I WILL MAKE you brooches and toys for your delight
Of bird-song at morning and star-shine at night.
I will make a palace fit for you and me,
Of green days in forests and blue days at sea.

I will make my kitchen, and you shall keep your room,
Where white flows the river and bright blows the broom,
And you shall wash your linen and keep your body white
In rainfall at morning and dewfall at night.

And this shall be for music when no one else is near,
The fine song for singing, the rare song to hear!
That only I remember, that only you admire,
Of the broad road that stretches and the roadside fire.

ROBERT LOUIS STEVENSON

William Butler Yeats (1865–1939)
Augustus John

The Lake Isle of Innisfree

I WILL ARISE and go now, and go to Innisfree,
And a small cabin build there, of clay and wattles made;
Nine bean rows will I have there, a hive for the honey bee,
    And live alone in the bee-loud glade.

And I shall have some peace there, for peace comes dropping slow,
Dropping from the veils of the morning to where the cricket sings;
There midnight's all a-glimmer, and noon a purple glow,
    And evening full of the linnet's wings.

I will arise and go now, for always night and day
I hear lake water lapping with low sounds by the shore;
While I stand on the roadway, or on the pavements gray,
    I hear it in the deep heart's core.

WILLIAM BUTLER YEATS

Rudyard Kipling (1865–1936)
John Collier

If

I F Y O U C A N keep your head when all about you
  Are losing theirs and blaming it on you,
If you can trust yourself when all men doubt you
But make allowance for their doubting too,
If you can wait and not be tired by waiting,
Or being lied about, don't deal in lies,
Or being hated, don't give way to hating,
And yet don't look too good, nor talk too wise:

If you can dream—and not make dreams your master,
If you can think—and not make thoughts your aim;
If you can meet with Triumph and Disaster
And treat those two impostors just the same;
If you can bear to hear the truth you've spoken
Twisted by knaves to make a trap for fools,
Or watch the things you gave your life to, broken,
And stoop and build 'em up with worn-out tools:

If you can make one heap of all your winnings
And risk it on one turn of pitch-and-toss,
And lose, and start again at your beginnings
And never breathe a word about your loss;
If you can force your heart and nerve and sinew
To serve your turn long after they are gone,
And so hold on when there is nothing in you
Except the Will which says to them: 'Hold on!'

If you can talk with crowds and keep your virtue,
Or walk with kings—nor lose the common touch,
If neither foes nor loving friends can hurt you;
If all men count with you, but none too much,
If you can fill the unforgiving minute
With sixty seconds' worth of distance run,
Yours is the Earth and everything that's in it,
And—which is more—you'll be a Man, my son!

RUDYARD KIPLING

acknowLedgements

Matthew Arnold (1822–88) (engraving) by English School, (19th century). Private Collection / Ken Welsh / The Bridgeman Art Library.

Aphra Behn (1640–89) (oil on canvas) by Lely, Sir Peter (1618–80). Yale Center for British Art, New Haven, USA / Bequest of Arthur D. Schlechter / The Bridgeman Art Library.

Miniature of William Blake (1757–1827) 1821 (w/c on ivory) by Linnell, John (1792–1882). Fitzwilliam Museum, University of Cambridge, UK / The Bridgeman Art Library.

Portrait of Robert Seymour Bridges (1844–1930) Poet Laureate (pencil on paper) by English School, (20th century). Corpus Christi College, Oxford, UK / The Bridgeman Art Library.

Portrait of Emily Brontë (1818–48) engraved by Walker and Boutall (engraving) by Brontë, Patrick Branwell (1817–48) (after). Private Collection / The Stapleton Collection / The Bridgeman Art Library.

Elizabeth Browning (1806–61) (engraving) by English School, (19th century). Private Collection / Ken Welsh / The Bridgeman Art Library.

Portrait of Robert Browning (1812–89), 1855 (w/c, pencil & coloured chalks on paper) by Rossetti, Dante Charles Gabriel (1828–82). Fitzwilliam Museum, University of Cambridge, UK / The Bridgeman Art Library.

Robert Burns (1759–96), 1787 by Nasmyth, Alexander (1758–1840). Scottish National Portrait Gallery, Edinburgh, Scotland / The Bridgeman Art Library.

Portrait of George Gordon (1788–1824) 6th Baron Byron of Rochdale in Albanian Dress, 1813 (oil on canvas) by Phillips, Thomas (1770–1845). National Portrait Gallery, London, UK / The Bridgeman Art Library.

Margaret Cavendish, Duchess of Newcastle (1624–74) (engraving) by English School, (17th century). Private Collection / The Bridgeman Art Library.

Portrait of John Clare (1793–1864) (engraving) (b/w photo) by Freeman, Samuel (1773–1857). Private Collection / The Bridgeman Art Library.

Samuel Taylor Coleridge, 1804 (oil on canvas) by Northcote, James (1746–1831). Wordsworth Trust / The Bridgeman Art Library.

William Congreve (1670–1729), engraved by John Faber (1684–1756), 1733 (engraving) by Kneller, Sir Godfrey (1646–1723) (after). City of Westminster Archive Centre, London, UK / The Bridgeman Art Library.

Portrait of William Cowper (1731–1800) (w/c on paper) by Blake, William (1757–1827). Ashmolean Museum, University of Oxford, UK / The Bridgeman Art Library.

Sir William Davenant (1606–68) (engraving) by English School, (17th century). Private Collection / The Bridgeman Art Library.

Portrait of John Donne, c.1595 (oil on canvas) by English School, (16th century). National Portrait Gallery, London, UK / The Bridgeman Art Library.

William Drummond of Hawthornden (1585–1649) 1609 (oil on panel) by Scottish School, (17th century). Scottish National Portrait Gallery, Edinburgh, Scotland / The Bridgeman Art Library.

John Dryden (1631–1700) engraved by William Faithorne (1616–91) (engraving) (b&w photo) by Closterman, Johann (1660–1711) (after). Private Collection / The Bridgeman Art Library.

Portrait of John Gay (1685–1732), author of The Beggar's Opera by Richardson, Jonathan (1665–1745). Gerald Coke Handel Collection, Foundling Museum, London / The Bridgeman Art Library.

Oliver Goldsmith (1730–74) (engraving) by English School, (19th century). Private Collection / Ken Welsh / The Bridgeman Art Library.

Portrait of Thomas Gray (1716–71) c.1731 (oil on canvas) by Pond, Arthur (c.1700–58) (attr. to). Fitzwilliam Museum, University of Cambridge, UK / The Bridgeman Art Library.

Portrait of Fulke Greville (1554–1628) 1st Baron Brooke, from 'Lodge's British Portraits', 1823 (engraving) by English School, (19th century). Private Collection / Ken Welsh / The Bridgeman Art Library.

George Herbert (1593–1633) (engraving) by English School, (17th century). Private Collection / Ken Welsh / The Bridgeman Art Library.

Robert Herrick (1591–1674), engraved by the artist (engraving) (b/w photo) by Marshall, William (fl.1617–49). Private Collection / The Bridgeman Art Library.

Dr. Samuel Johnson (1709–84) 1775 (oil on canvas) by Reynolds, Sir Joshua (1723–92). Private Collection / The Bridgeman Art Library.

Ben Jonson (1573–1637), engraved by George Vertue (1684–1756), 1730 (engraving) by Honthorst, Gerrit van (1590–1656) (after). City of Westminster Archive Centre, London, UK / The Bridgeman Art Library.

A portrait miniature of John Keats (1795–1821) c.1818 (ivory) by Severn, Joseph (1793–1879). Fitzwilliam Museum, University of Cambridge, UK / The Bridgeman Art Library.

Rudyard Kipling (1865–1936), 1891 (oil on canvas) by Collier, John (1850–1934). Bateman's, Burwash, East Sussex, UK / National Trust Photographic Library / John Hammond / The Bridgeman Art Library.

Portrait of Charles Lamb (1775–1834) 1826 (oil on canvas) by English School, (19th century). National Portrait Gallery, London, UK / The Bridgeman Art Library.

Mary Ann Lamb (1764–1867) illustration from 'Little Journeys to the Homes of Famous Women', published 1897 (litho) by English School, (19th century). Private Collection / Ken Welsh / The Bridgeman Art Library.

Andrew Marvell (1621–78), engraved by John Raphael Smith (1752–1812) (engraving) (b&w photo) by English School, (17th century). Private Collection / The Bridgeman Art Library.

George Meredith (1828–1909) (oil on canvas) (b/w photo) by English School, (19th century). Private Collection / The Bridgeman Art Library.

Portrait bust of John Milton (1608–74) (marble) by English School, (18th century). Private Collection / Lawrence Steigrad Fine Arts, New York / The Bridgeman Art Library.

A Woman called Lady Mary Wortley Montagu, c.1715–20 (oil on canvas) by Kneller, Sir Godfrey (1646–1723). Yale Center for British Art, Paul Mellon Collection, USA / The Bridgeman Art Library.

Thomas Love Peacock (1785–1866) (b/w photo). Private Collection / The Bridgeman Art Library.

Alexander Pope and his dog, Bounce, c.1718 by Richardson, Jonathan (1665–1745) (attr. to). Private Collection / The Bridgeman Art Library.

Mrs. Mary Robinson (Perdita) 1783–84 (oil on canvas) by Reynolds, Sir Joshua (1723–92). Wallace Collection, London, UK / The Bridgeman Art Library.

Christina Georgina Rossetti (1830–94) illustration from 'Little Journeys to the Homes of Famous Women', published 1897 (litho) by Rossetti, Dante Gabriel (1828–82) (after). Private Collection / Ken Welsh / The Bridgeman Art Library.

Portrait of Sir Walter Scott (oil on canvas) by Grant, Sir Francis (1803–78). City of Edinburgh Museums and Art Galleries, Scotland / The Bridgeman Art Library.

Titlepage of 'Mr. William Shakespeares Comedies, Histories and Tragedies', engraved by Martin Droeshout (1601–50) 1623 (see also 54369) by English School, (17th century). British Library, London, UK / Giraudon / The Bridgeman Art Library.

Portrait of Percy Bysshe Shelley, 1819 (oil on canvas) by Curran, Amelia (1775–1847). National Portrait Gallery, London, UK / The Bridgeman Art Library.

Portrait of a gentleman, said to be Edmund Spenser (c.1552–99), the Kinnoull Portrait (panel) by English School, (17th century). Private Collection / Philip Mould Ltd, London / The Bridgeman Art Library.

Portrait of Robert Louis Stevenson (1850–1894) 1886 (oil on canvas) by Richmond, Sir William Blake (1842–1921). National Portrait Gallery, London, UK / The Bridgeman Art Library.

Portrait of Algernon Charles Swinburne (1837–1909) (oil on canvas) by Scott, William Bell (1811–90). Balliol College, Oxford, UK / The Bridgeman Art Library.

Lord Alfred Tennyson (1809–92), 1901 (oil) by Hambidge, Alice (1869–1947). Private Collection / The Maas Gallery, London, UK / The Bridgeman Art Library.

Anne Wharton, illustration from 'A catalogue of Royal and Noble Authors, Volume III', published in 1806 (colour litho) by English School, (19th century). Private Collection / Ken Welsh / The Bridgeman Art Library.

John Wilmot (1647–80) 2nd Earl of Rochester, c.1675 (oil on canvas) by Huysmans, Jacob (c.1633–96) (attr. to). Warwick Castle, Warwickshire / The Bridgeman Art Library.

Portrait of William Wordsworth (1770–1850) 1842 (oil on canvas) by Haydon, Benjamin Robert (1786–1846). National Portrait Gallery, London, UK/ Giraudon / The Bridgeman Art Library.

Sir Thomas Wyatt (c.1503–42) engraved by Francesco Bartolozzi (1727–1815) (engraving) by Holbein, Hans the Younger (1497/8–1543) (after). Private Collection / The Stapleton Collection / The Bridgeman Art Library.

William Butler Yeats (1865–1939) 1930 (oil on canvas) by John, Augustus Edwin (1878–1961). Art Gallery and Museum, Kelvingrove, Glasgow, Scotland / Glasgow City Council (Museums) / The Bridgeman Art Library.